Be What You Are

As the Solution lies within You

Be Your Own Hero - Nothing is Impossible for us,

Dedicated to all my Readers!!!

There is a famous Quote from Bhagavad Gita

"Man is made by his belief, as he believes, so he is"

Sometimes the only thing which can make you win is your courage, your belief in you, your Self – Consciousness.

"It's Never Late to Be What You Might Have Been"

<u>*Disclaimer*</u>

Abhinandan Asthana asserts the moral rights to be identified as the author of this work. In this book writer has tried to explain the concept of Self – Motivation, Will Power and concepts of Personality Development in easy and example-oriented way.

Author tried to make this book more interesting for the reader by adding some fictional characters and making the story really near to the real-life scenarios.

Somewhere the book is inspired by true events, the names, characters and incidents in it are the products of author's imagination.

Any resemblance to the actual person living or dead or localities is entirely coincidental, due care has been taken while editing and printing the book.

Neither Author nor publisher of the book holds any responsibility for any mistake that may have crept inadvertently.

1

Art of Self- Motivation

"Just Because You Took Longer than others doesn't mean that you failed"

Start with the golden lines which we normally miss in our lives and keep on cursing our situation that if this was good that has happened and if that has happened and blah blah blah….

I am definitely not going to share any motivational goals or target to you, but in coming pages you are going to identify the hidden treasure in yourself the golden art of *Self- Motivation*.

And definitely you are going to learn the benefits of *"Being What You Are"* in context of long terms goal achievement in your Life.

I am going to change your opinion of seeing the world around you, I am going to change the way you handle the difficult situations in your life and possibly I am going to change your attitude towards by your inner power of *"Being What You Are"*.

Self – Motivation

The best kind of motivation is self-motivation.

You might not be intimately familiar with the term "self-motivation" but you almost certainly know this to be true.

Think about two separate experiences you have no doubt had:

Scenario 1: You have something you "have to do." You're not excited or passionate about it, but you know you need to get it done all the same, so you work hard to complete your task.

Scenario 2: You have something you "get to do." You're interested in your task—you may have even set this task for yourself rather than receiving it from someone else—and you are happy to put in the time and effort to complete it.

In which scenario are you more effective? In which scenario are you more efficient? In which scenario do you feel the most fulfilled?

I'm willing to bet that your answer to each of those questions is **"Scenario 2."**

It won't come as a surprise to you that doing something for its own sake and for your own purposes is likely to be more fulfilling, more enjoyable, and more successful than doing something to meet external standards or to please others.

The feeling you have in **Scenario 2** is that of being *"Self-Motivated."* Read on to learn more about self-motivation and why it's so much more effective than the motivation in **Scenario 1.**

"Push Yourself as no one is going to do it for You"

Now the question arises:

What does the Self – Motivation means?

You probably already know what self-motivation is, but just in case your idea of what is it needs a bit of fleshing out, here's a good definition:

"Self-motivation is, in its simplest form, the force that drives you to do things." (Skills You Need, n.d.).

It's the drive you have to work towards your goals, put effort into self-development, and achieve personal fulfillment.

It's important to note here that self-motivation is generally driven by intrinsic motivation, or the motivation to achieve that comes from sincerely wanting to achieve and desiring the inherent rewards associated.

It can also be driven by extrinsic motivation, the drive to achieve that comes from wanting the external rewards (like money, power, status, or recognition), although it's clear that intrinsic motivation is usually a more effective and fulfilling drive.

Here let's learn 2 terms which we always hear,

EI → Emotional Intelligence

SM → Self-Motivation

The two most important and relative factors, don't worry I am going to explain it in very easy language.

According to an Emotional Intelligence expert, Self-motivation is a key component of Emotional intelligence. Emotional intelligence is the measure of an individual's ability to recognize and manage their emotions and the emotions of other people.

The placement of self-motivation within emotional intelligence highlights its role within our ability to understand ourselves, relate to others, and to succeed in reaching our goals.

There are four components of motivation:

- Achievement drive, or the personal drive to achieve, improve, and meet certain standards.
- Commitment to your own personal goals.
- Initiative, or the "readiness to act on opportunities."

- Optimism, the tendency to look ahead and persevere with the belief that you can reach your goals.

"No Matter how hard it is, no matter how hard it gets, I am going to do it"

Self-motivation is easy to understand when you consider some examples:

> A man who goes to work every day just to pay the bills, keep his family off his back, and please his boss is not self-motivated, while a man who needs no external forces to make the trek into work every day and finds fulfillment in what he does is self-motivated.

> The student who only completes her homework when her parents remind her, nag her, or ground her for failure to complete is not self-motivated, but the student who completes her homework with no prodding because she wants to learn and succeed in school is self-motivated.

> The woman who only goes to the gym when her friends drag her there or because her doctor is adamant that she needs to exercise to get healthy again is not self-motivated, but the woman who sets an early alarm and schedules time to get to the gym whether anyone encourages her or not is self-motivated.

As you can see, self-motivation is all about where your drive comes from; if your motivation comes from within and pushes you to achieve for your own personal reasons, it can be considered self-motivation.

If you are only motivated to achieve standards set by someone else and not for your own internal satisfaction, you are probably not self-motivated.

It's possible to be self-motivated in some areas of life and not in others. For example, if the man from the first example is not internally motivated to go to work but is sure to make time for his marathon training, he is not self-motivated when it comes to work but may be self-motivated regarding his training.

The Importance of Self-Motivation

As you have likely guessed already, Self-Motivation is an important concept; while we are certainly capable of getting things done to please others and meet external standards, these efforts are not what we would call a "labor of love."

In other words, doing things because we feel we have to do them or to gain some external reward is enough in many cases, but it doesn't invoke the passion that drives innovation and excellence.

It's fine to use external sources to motivate you in some areas, but if you're not doing anything that's self-motivated, you are unlikely to feel personally fulfilled and to find deeper meaning in your life.

Not only do we generally do better work when we are self-motivated, we are also better able to cope with stress and simply happier when we are doing what we want to be doing.

"Find the place inside yourself where nothing is Impossible"

Some tips and skills for Self – Motivation:

- ➤ Setting high but realistic goals (e.g., SMART goals).
- ➤ Taking the right level of risk.
- ➤ Seeking constant feedback to figure out how to improve.
- ➤ Being committed to personal goals and going "the extra mile" to achieve them.
- ➤ Actively seeking out opportunities and seizing them when they occur.
- ➤ The ability to deal with setbacks and continue in pursuing your goals despite obstacles (i.e., resilience).

> ➢ Continue learning and acquiring knowledge (i.e., develop a love of learning).
> ➢ Spend time with motivated, enthusiastic, and supportive people.
> ➢ Cultivate a positive mindset and work on your optimism and resilience.
> ➢ Identify your strengths and weaknesses, and work on them.
> ➢ Avoid procrastination and work on your time management skills.
> ➢ Get help when you need it, and be willing to help others succeed.

"When You Feel like Quitting, Think Back Why You Started"

2

Art of Saying "No"

"I don't know the key to success, but key to failure is to please everybody"

While the origin of humanity might stem from a single source, the truth of the matter is that, today, we are all different. We live different lives, have different beliefs, values, relationships, thoughts and emotions. We raise our children differently, think differently and behave differently on a number of levels.

Although common threads might join us, we are all unique in our own little ways. And since we are all unique, with unique points of view and ways of doing things, oftentimes, we consider our own way as the right way of going about things. Because of that, it's easy to understand why we're critical of others. That could also be why it's impossible to please everyone in life.

That might be the reason why people disapprove of our decisions. That might be the reason why, no matter what you do, think or feel, someone will act dismayed or feel disgruntled by the very notion of your choices or your existence even.

How could they possibly think that way or say those things or behave in such a manner?

Clearly, you can't please everyone. It's downright impossible. From how you speak to your child, to what types of clothes you wear, what you do for work, the decisions you make on where and what to eat, how you drive your car, spend your money, and everything in between, someone is going to disapprove.

Why You Shouldn't Try to Please Everyone?

You absolutely shouldn't try to please everyone all the time. It's just not worth it. Not only will you begin to live your life according to someone else's standards, but you'll deplete yourself of any sense of happiness or enthusiasm.

Do what makes you happy and what pleases you. As long as you're doing the right things with a good heart, that's all that really matters.

It's hard to stay this course when you know that people are talking behind your back, or even in front of your face. People tend to enjoy saying things that hurt others.

For one reason or another, it helps to elevate their egos and empower their bold personalities. It's hard to turn the other cheek while people smite you on both sides. But you simply have to.

"Be Yourself and Be Happy"

There are a number of reasons why it's impossible to please everyone, and while this information might not completely alleviate your worries, reduce your stress, or eliminate all your fears for pursuing your dreams, it will hopefully allow you to come to the realization that nobody will be completely pleased with your actions all the time.

What's important is that you do you. Don't concern yourself with what others think you should do. Don't allow that to impact the trajectory of your hopes and your dreams.

Don't allow that to diminish your spirit or change your direction of travel when it's something that you're deeply passionate about or have always wanted to do in your life.

Never give up on your hopes and your dreams just because you're trying to make others happy around you. To a certain extent, our family's happiness is important.

So is the happiness of our friends. But not beyond the extent that we start self-sacrificing all that we've ever wanted and hoped for in life.

Don't allow peer pressure to hold you back. Set your goals sky high. You can achieve anything you put your mind to. It doesn't matter what other people say or think about you.

As long as you're doing what makes you happy, that's what's important. As long as, deep down inside, you're sated, and you're doing things for the right reasons with the right motivations, you should never feel sorry for it.

And while there might be dozens of reasons why it's impossible to please everyone, there are 10 that are truly important. They cut down to the core of who we are.

They help to highlight the importance of our own hopes and dreams, rather than trying to live some fabricated life just to please the other people that are around us. Never do that. Never.

"Everyone will always have an opinion no matter what"

No matter what you do or how hard you try, people will always have an opinion about you. Often, it's a negative opinion. They look at you with distaste and scorn.

You can't please those people no matter what you do. You can't avoid them from talking and gossiping about you behind your back or even right in front of your face. And you shouldn't bother trying either.

Nothing will ever change the thoughts and minds of others that are steeped in negativity. Nothing you ever do can please them. It's quite literally impossible.

So why bother trying? They will have an opinion about how you live your life, because it's different from some Utopian ideals they have envisioned in their minds.

"Right and wrong can often be subjective"

I'm not talking about moral issues here. I'm not talking about murder or robbery or anything else that's illegal in the eyes of the law. However, all of that aside, right and wrong can be almost entirely subjective.

What's right in one person's mind, could be wrong in another person's mind.

Most things are considered subjective. They're open to interpretation. There isn't a set way of doing every single thing in life that's always the right way.

Because of that, people will differ in their opinions of just how to approach something. If you're not doing it their way, how can you expect to please them and everyone else for that matter?

"We are all the unique product of our own experiences"

No two people are exactly alike. Physically speaking, two twins might be completely identical, but their personalities are shaped differently. They are unique in their own special little ways.

If two identical twins can be so different, how do you expect other people who are from different cultures and upbringings to be so similar?

Since we are all the unique product of our own experiences, and we all share different values and beliefs, we behave differently. Even someone you might think you know quite well might have a hidden value or belief that reveals itself when you do something that disobeys or runs in contrast to their particular thoughts.

"People will always talk no matter what you decide to do"

The nature of humanity is to talk. We talk about others in an attempt to feel better about ourselves. Gossip is quite possibly one of the worst ways to pass the time.

There's no sense in gossiping. If you're partaking in gossiping on a regular basis, then you're filling your life with negativity rather than positivity. It's harder to push past the status quo when you live in the negative realm.

Considering that people will always talk, there's not much you can do to please those people. They will always find something about you to talk about. That's just the nature of groups and clicks.

They're almost cult-like in their nature. They feed off of negativity and seeing others hurt. But you simply have to ignore it. Develop thick skin and turn the other cheek.

"Outcasts and scapegoats are a common theme throughout history"

People have always shunned others, out casting them amongst society to prove that they're better than these people. This is also something that tends to happen when famous people fail or hit rock bottom, get arrested or any other number of things.

Throughout history, we like to see those at the top come crashing down.

For some reason, this invigorates the human spirit. We revel in the failure of others. It's an unfortunate truth. We also use scapegoats to help reason away certain things.

With all this in mind, it's clear that it's impossible to please these people. It's impossible to ever appease all of them at the same time. So, you shouldn't try.

"People are usually frightened by things they don't understand"

Whatever you want out of life, whatever dreams or desires you might have, not everyone around you is going to understand them. In fact, some are likely to be frightened by them.

When one person in a group begins to succeed while the others remain within the status quo, there's a certain amount of tension that's created.

People are usually frightened by what they don't understand. Since your journey is unique, you can't expect everyone to understand it. And you also can't expect that every action you take or decision you make to please everyone.

It simply won't happen. But don't let it dissuade you from confidently marching towards your goals.

"If your dreams don't scare you, they aren't big enough"

We're often afraid of not pleasing everyone around us when we have big hopes and dreams for the future. We worry about what others might think.

We worry about how others might judge us and feel about us. How will the people closest to us react? What will they say when we expose our innermost desires to them?

The truth is that if your dreams don't scare you, they aren't big enough. It shouldn't matter what other people will say or think as long as it's something you're passionate about.

You shouldn't try to please every single person because it will literally be impossible to do it. But don't compromise your dreams for others. Get out there and pursue them with all your heart.

"When you try to please everyone, you end up attracting negativity"

The Law of Attraction is powerful. We don't realize that we attract whatever is in our minds. Like begets like. That's also why we tend to move towards our greatest fears.

We have a tendency for attracting those things into our lives that are at the forefronts of our minds. And when you try to please everyone, you simply end up attracting more negativity.

You can't please them all. So be careful with where your mind is at. Be careful on the things that you're thinking or saying on a daily basis. Since 45% of our behaviour is habit driven, it's difficult to always notice the habits that are holding us back.

"You begin to sacrifice who you really are deep down inside"

When you try to please everyone, you end up sacrificing who you really are deep down inside. You end up going against the grain of the things that you've always wanted in life.

When you do that, you suffer over the long term, having regrets and replaying those what-ifs and should-haves in your mind over and over again.

Don't allow other peoples' opinions of you to stop you from doing what you really love. You can't please them all. If you really want to pursue something, even if you've failed a number of times and even if people have spoken negatively about you in the past, do it.

Do it for you. Don't do it for them. Do it because it's what you really want out of life.

"You will lose a sense of your identity by trying to please others"

When we try to please others all the time, we lose ourselves. We lose our identities. The things that we used to hold near and dear are all but forgotten.

We live a life of conformity, trying to adapt to the will of others who pressure us into doing things that please them rather than that please us.

You should pursue your dreams no matter what. If you don't want to risk losing any semblance of your own identity, don't give up hope. There is light at the other end of the tunnel.

Don't put all your dreams on hold just because you're trying to please all the other people around you.

That's Why the Title says **"Be What You Are"**

3

Decoding Happiness

"Lying brings Short Term Happiness with Long Term Pain,

Honesty brings Long Term Happiness with Short Term Pain"

Elements of Short-Term Happiness:

Humour

Entertainment

Surprise

Pleasure (Food, Sex, Relaxation)

Elements of Long-Term Happiness

Meaning & Purpose

Fulfilment

Inspiration

Long - Lasting Love

The single biggest pitfall in the pursuit of happiness is the pursuit of short-term happiness instead of long-term happiness. This tendency towards instant gratification and small hits of happiness are one of the biggest reasons for unhappiness in the current scenario.

With all the resources at our disposal, we choose to pursue short term goals that will make us happy for an instant, but leave us feeling empty and constantly yearning for more over the long run.

How short term is short-term?

It can be very short term, and not even that happy. For example, short term happiness can come from purchasing a new big screen TV. This will make you happy for little while as you show off to your friends how great Movies looks in HD, but eventually you won't derive anymore happiness from the television.

On the flip side, short term happiness can be derived from something as trivial as checking your phone every time it pings ("Oh, my phone vibrated. I feel important!").

In order to understand why we tend to prioritize short term happiness over long term happiness, we need to understand a bit of the science.

You see, short term happiness usually results in a short burst of dopamine being released in our brains. Dopamine is the happy hormone. It's what makes us feel good. Our brain releases dopamine with certain triggers. The triggers can be as big as finish a marathon, or as small as checking your phone.

The reason short term happiness is so dangerous is because it trains us to chase constant hits of dopamine. For instance, buying a new pair of shoes can trigger a dopamine hit, and a temporary satisfaction.

However, that dopamine doesn't last. But we remember it. And we want it again.

So, what do we do?

We repeat the behaviour that made us feel that way the first time around, and we end up with entire rooms full of shoes.

Chasing short term happiness turns us into happiness junkies just looking for that next dopamine hit. Incidentally, drugs and alcohol also cause temporary spikes in dopamine, which is part of what makes them addictive.

The moment the high is over, you're chasing the next high, and so you embark on the happiness treadmill, where you never actually reach your destination, which is always just out of reach.

A few common examples of short-term happiness include alcohol and drugs, but also shopping, and keeping up appearances. Consumerist culture is founded on short term happiness.

Chasing these short bursts of happiness constantly is stressful. As a result, we end up developing anxiety about the way we live, constantly worrying about where our next hit is going to come from.

Short term happiness junkies are addicts. Pure and simple. And it could very well be the most rampant addiction in the developed world.

There's only one solution: focus on long term happiness. If you put yourself on the path to fulfilling all of your needs (financial, physical, mental, emotional and spiritual), you can get off the happiness treadmill, relieve yourself of your anxiety, kick your addiction, and ultimately live a truly happy life.

"Short - Term discomforts are stepping stone for Long – Term Happiness"

How happy are you?

Happiness is becoming a huge area in psychological research and even in government policy, exploring a "happiness index". It's tough, though, to define exactly what happiness is, and what makes us happy.

There are two broad ways of looking at happiness, though: short-term happiness (a great cookie, a bottle of wine) and long-term happiness (financial security, achieving your goals).

Both types of happiness are valid, and important. The problem is, they're often in competition.

Let's say you've got a goal of losing 50lbs this year. You know you'd be happier and healthier if you weren't carrying that extra weight. To achieve long-term happiness, you need to go on a diet.

In the short-term, though, it's not that easy. A slab of chocolate cake, or a large glass of wine, might seem like just the thing to cheer you up at the end of a long day - or to celebrate with friends.

It's the same with lots of other goals. Perhaps you want to save up money for a fantastic holiday abroad in five-year time - but in the short term, that means cutting back on eating out and buying new DVDs.

Or maybe you're trying to get qualified for a new career - something that would make you much happier in the future, but that requires a lot of hard work right now.

Looking to the Long-Term

Most of us find it much easier to see immediate rewards - and consequences - than ones which are years away.

If you want to achieve your goals over months or years, try:

- Creating a vision board or another visual reminder of your goals, so that they're constantly in front of you
- Breaking your dream into smaller steps, so that you've got something more immediate to focus on
- Writing down your reasons for pursuing this goal, so you can go back to your list whenever your motivation flags

Don't pin all your hopes of happiness on some far-off future, though.

There's no point working a 60-hour week and making yourself thoroughly miserable in the belief that things will be perfect as soon as you're making a six-figure salary.

Life is for Living - Right Now

If you've got a tendency to prioritize long-term happiness at the expense of day-to-day pleasures, then start looking for some small ways to bring a little joy back into your life.

I'm not suggesting that you go out and get drunk every night, or that you stuff yourself with cake or go on a spending spree. There are plenty of other ways to enjoy yourself.

How about,

- Setting a budget for discretionary spending, so that you can buy magazines, computer games, books or whatever it is you enjoy.
- Looking for forms of exercises that you find fun - exercise boosts your mood right now, but also improves your health over weeks, months and years
- Giving yourself time each day for leisure activities. (And I know TV gets a bad rap, but I personally think there's nothing wrong with watching your favourite show once in a while.)

Of course, the best activities are ones that you enjoy right now, but that also help you build a happier future.

4

Fighting Fear of Failures and Rejections

Fear has two meanings -

Forget Everything and Run

or

Face Everything and Rise

Choice is Yours

Our need for achievement is inborn, it's a reflection of the human ability to process information, form plans, and solve problems. It helps us get a sense of control over our environment and life challenges.

Our fear of failure, however, seems to be learned. It is the result of being teased or shamed whenever our achievements fall short.

But here's the thing—we're always falling short because we can never know everything or control everything.

What we have been calling failure is usually part of the inevitable human condition.

If you are going through life changes or problems that you can't control, like infertility, rethink that failure label. The problem may be a disappointment, even a shock, but it is not a personal failure.

It is hard enough that you may be dealing with a major problem and blaming yourself and thinking any part of your problem means you're a failure is adding insult to injury.

Instead of using the word failure, try using the word inconvenient. It is more realistic, and it is time to get real.

Expecting yourself to anticipate, prevent, and cure all life problems is not real. It's a fantasy and the fear of failure makes coping and risk-taking more difficult in two ways.

"The Greatest Hindrance to Success is the Fear of Failure"

First, the fear of failure undermines your natural need for achievement behaviour. When you are dealing with infertility, or any diagnosis or crisis, moving towards a goal is the only way to achieve a solution or resolution. Fear of failure keeps you defensive and frozen in place instead of moving forward.

Second, fear of failure encourages you to do things the hard way, so you have an excuse for others if you fail.

For example, if you do all your studying for a test the night before instead of all semester long, you have given yourself an excuse for failure.

You probably had to study twice as hard and lose a night's sleep and feel overwhelmed with anxiety, but you now have an excuse for failure. When it comes to fertility treatment, however, do it the easy way. Don't wait. If you've tried on your own for a year without success, reach out for information and a fertility specialist.

You need help, not excuses.

Inside every human being is a desire to pursue wild ambitions and discover new possibilities. There's a would-be entrepreneur, motivational speaker, freelance writer, stage performer, or off-the-grid traveller in all of us.

But unfortunately, most people spend their lives in a routine, nondescript comfort zone because they're too intimidated to chase a goal that seems uncertain and prone to fail.

According to a survey, an estimated 80% employees in Corporate Sector in India including IT are not interested in their job and doing only for paying bills.

The most common is a fear of personal failure, which most of us define broadly as unemployment, financial ruin, and isolation from others.

Also called *"atychiphobia,"* this fear of failure often becomes so debilitating it can hinder a person from attempting any goal that is not a guaranteed success.

It feels safe and secure, but functioning in this state of rigidity will hold you back from opportunities, experiences and overall happiness.

Here are five potential indicators that a fear of failure has come between you and the life of purpose, excitement, or satisfaction you dream about.

You Procrastinate or Avoid Responsibility

Did you know there's a direct correlation between the fear of failure and a person's ability to manage assignments within the time allotted?

Those who panic at the idea of failing exhibit a lower sense of self-determination that often causes a lack of motivation to finish deadline-driven projects.

It squelches the confidence to take on major responsibilities. If you feel immobilized to perform tasks out of concern that you won't succeed, this fear of failure can inhibit your productivity.

You Feel Discontent in Your Career Path

At some point in your career, you'll feel disengaged and antsy, ready for something new, but paralyzed without knowing where your next step should be.

A report says that job dissatisfaction rates are well above 80 percent, but that most people are unlikely to quit a current profession and seek out their real passion instead. This trend to a behaviour known as "risk-aversion."

This theory of risk aversion suggests individuals are conditioned to choose safety and familiarity over ambiguity and unpredictability, often to the detriment of their own happiness.

If you allow extreme caution to keep you stuck in a mediocre or creatively stifling position, this fear of failure can stagnate your career growth.

You Worry About Disappointing Others

Those who define failure in terms of letting others down ignore their own aspirations because they're too focused on cooperating with the opinions of everyone else.

Too much emphasis on outside voices will deter a person from experiencing fulfilment and authenticity. If you avoid disappointment, this fear of failure can harm both your relationships and self-awareness.

You Experience Physical Effects of Stress

When people spend all of their energy fixating on the possibility of defeat, they risk suffering both physically and mentally.

Our bodies manifest stress and anxiety in a wide variety of ways, including panic attacks, headaches, sweating, muscle spasms, insomnia, and gastrointestinal distress.

An outward sign of anxiety should not be disregarded, but rather, taken care of before it escalates into a more serious condition. If you have extreme reactions to stress, this fear of failure can jeopardize your health over time.

You Aren't Proactive About Your Future

People tend to over analyse future events because they're unable to predict what might happen. This pattern leads to feeling powerless.

Without immediate assurance and instant gratification, the unknown becomes a source of distress for many individuals. If you sidestep thoughts, plans or conversations about the future, this fear of failure can sabotage both your current goals and future prospects or opportunities.

Before you can overcome a phobia, it's crucial to understand the reason it exists in the first place. Once you commit to taking risks that are important to you, you'll discover a stronger, bolder, and happier version of yourself.

Consequences of Fear of Failure:

Everyone hates to fail, but for some people, failing presents such a significant psychological threat their motivation to avoid failure exceeds their motivation to succeed.

This fear of failure causes them to unconsciously sabotage their chances of success, in a variety of ways.

Failing can elicit feelings such as disappointment, anger, frustration, sadness, regret, and confusion that, while unpleasant, are usually not sufficient to trigger a full-blown fear of failure.

Indeed, the term is somewhat of a misnomer because it is not failure per se that underlies the behaviour of people who have it. Rather, a fear of failure is essentially a fear of shame.

People who have a fear of failure are motivated to avoid failing not because they cannot manage the basic emotions of disappointment, anger, and frustration that accompany such experiences but because failing also makes them feel deep shame.

Shame is a psychologically toxic emotion because instead of feeling bad about our actions (guilt) or our efforts (regret), shame makes us feel bad who we are.

Shame gets to the core of our egos, our identities, our self-esteem, and our feelings of emotional well-being. The damaging nature of shame makes it urgent for those who have a fear of failure to avoid the psychological threats associated with failing by finding unconscious ways to mitigate the implications of a potential failure.

For example, by buying unnecessary new clothes for a job interview instead of reading up on the company—which allows them to use the excuse, "I just didn't have time to fully prepare."

Signs You Might Have a Fear of Failure

- Failing makes you worry about what other people think about you.
- Failing makes you worry about your ability to pursue the future you desire.
- Failing makes you worry that people will lose interest in you.
- Failing makes you worry about how smart or capable you are.
- Failing makes you worry about disappointing people whose opinion you value.
- You tend to tell people beforehand that you don't expect to succeed in order to lower their expectations.
- Once you fail at something, you have trouble imagining what you could have done differently to succeed.

- You often get last-minute headaches, stomach aches, or other physical symptoms that prevent you from completing your preparation.
- You often get distracted by tasks that prevent you from completing your preparation which, in hindsight, were not as urgent as they seemed at the time.
- You tend to procrastinate and "run out of time" to complete your preparation adequately.

Try these strategies for unlearning fear of failure:

- Focus on gathering information—not other people's opinions about you or your choices.

- Look at all situations involving your goals through your own eyes only—spectating (looking at yourself through others' eyes to see if you look like a failure) will drain time and energy and will probably be inaccurate anyway.

- Understand that falling short of a goal is a learning experience—a failed fertility treatment cycle gives you and your physician more data.

- A reaction to a hormone injection gives you data about your body's autoimmune system. This means every try, even ones that don't score a goal, are small successes.

- Describe your behaviour to yourself, don't judge it— ***"I am who I am"*** and ***"It is what it is"*** are great mantras since our feelings are influenced by our thinking, and we can choose what we say to ourselves.

- Try your best, but don't put yourself on trial—self-blaming feeds the fear of failure. To counteract the fear of failure, practice thinking of yourself as your defence lawyer, not the lawyer for the prosecution.

Failure is a part of life. Fear of failure doesn't have to be. So, choose not to let fear gets in your way. If you are not failing at least 25 percent of the time, you are not taking enough chances or setting enough goals. Go for it!

5

Decoding Life

Few lines from Bhagavad Gita

*"If things are happening as per your wish then you are lucky, but
if the things are not happening as per your wish then you are very
lucky as it's happening as per the God's wish"*

**Have you noticed that your life doesn't always turn out the way
you want?**

In fact, more often than not, you don't get what you want.

Or.

You don't get what you think you want.

This is a good thing.

Its life nudging you in the right direction.

Its life showing you where you need to grow, and what you need to release, to become the person you are meant to be.

The problem then isn't that life is hard, but something entirely different.

But before we get to that, let's ask ourselves an important question.

Why is Life So Hard?

It's hard because:

You think it's hard.

Your expectations are out of alignment with reality.

You're not following what makes your heart sing.

There are times when I feel like I want to give up. I feel like the universe is against me.

I just want to leave everything. I dream about the freedom I would have if I didn't have to do anything.

But then I remember something.

I remember that I'm doing what I'm doing because I've chosen this. I'm living my passion. I've chosen to follow the magnetic pull of life. That doesn't mean it's always easy.

I've also discovered to not take myself seriously when I have a bad day. The way it works for me is that I'll feel a tight feeling in my chest. Sometimes I feel emotional, sometimes overwhelmed, sometimes life just seems blah.

That then gives rise to thoughts that reflect what I'm feeling. I start looking at my business and life. I start searching for problems that I can fix.

In the past, I would chase these phantoms, thinking that fixing something would alleviate my inner turmoil.

Today, I take a step back.

I relax, I watch a movie, I meditate, and I remember to breathe. And I know that this too will pass, and it does.

A famous quote on hardness of life,

"Smoother Roads Never Makes Good Drivers, Problems Free Life Never Makes Strong Man, So Never Say to life Why Me say Try Me!"

The Art of Living Life,

- If you want to live a happy life, you have to be okay with being unhappy.
- Life goes up and down. You experience joy, and you experience pain. This is life. And this is okay.
- You don't need to hold on so tight. You don't have to make life do what you think you want.
- In short, you have to let go of wanting to control everything.

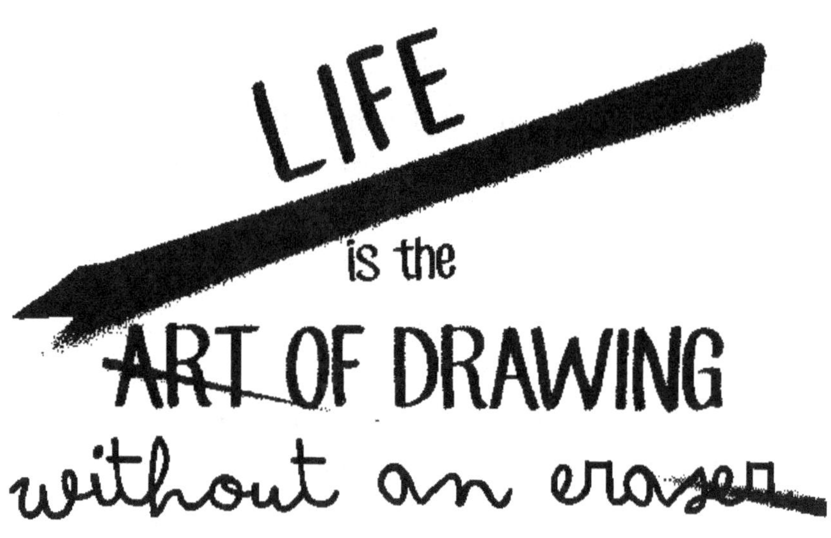

Here are four effective tips for when you feel like life is against you:

- Realize that life is full of challenges. It will constantly throw new problems at you. This is good. It's exciting. If it didn't happen, you'd stop growing and life would become bland. Just look at the people who've given up on life and settled for comfort. They're bored out of their mind.

- Examine your expectations. Do you expect amazing results even when you're a complete beginner at something? If you're just starting to uncover your passion and build your business, expect trouble, and go at your own pace. Trust your inner authority.

- Remember that happiness comes from the inside. It's not up to life or anyone outside of you to make you happy. You make yourself happy or unhappy through the thoughts you believe. Why do you think people experience the same event in different ways? It's an inside job. I'm not saying control your thoughts. I'm saying relax, and let the dance do its thing.

- Surround yourself with like-minded people. So, make sure you surround yourself with positive, friendly people who have the same goals as you do. It doesn't matter whether it's online or offline.

Life doesn't always turn out the way you want, but so what?

It doesn't matter. Every time something "goes wrong" is a reminder that you need to take a break and look inside.

Why are you suffering? Why do you believe the stories your mind weaves?

"We must be willing to let go of the life we planned so as to have the life that is waiting for us."

When I let go of how I think life should be, and listen to my heart, I open myself up to what's right here, right now.

The Bottom Line,

When life doesn't go your way, look at what it's trying to tell you.

Are you going after what you truly want, or are you living life on someone else's terms?

When you start following your heart, your life will change.

This doesn't mean things will be easy. If anything, life sometimes gets harder, because you have to face your inner demons.

You have to go against the status quo.

But you don't have to try and get somewhere, or become someone to feel good. Everything is fine and dandy in its messiness.

You're on a journey. You will always keep growing, evolving, falling flat on your face, and learning.

The key then is not to try and fix life, but to learn to relate to life in a new way.

"You are not meant to understand life. You are meant to live it."

Living the Life, You Want to Live is No Mystery

"The truth is, most people aren't living an extraordinary life. They're drifting through life without really knowing where they're going or what they want. As a result, their relationships, income, health, activities, and behaviours are pretty mediocre."

Most people aren't living the life they want to live.

They aren't following the path they dreamed of and they'll likely never live the life they want because they aren't willing to make it happen for themselves.

But this doesn't have to be you.

Living the life, you want to live is no mystery if you take the right steps.

Define Your Own Success

"*Define success on your own terms, achieve it by your own rules, and build a life you're proud to live.*"

You cannot live the life you want to live if you go on to believing that success is what everyone else says it is.

You must do the things you want to do and achieve the success you want to achieve in order for it to mean something.

I'll tell you, I'm learning this the hard way.

Leaving high school, I like a lot of other individuals I had no idea what I wanted to do for the rest of my life.

I saw university was the path everyone was naturally taking, so I thought: "Hell, I'll do the same."

I had the idea of being either an architect, lawyer or accountant. I thought the lives those guys were living looked pretty good, why not give up 3 years of my life to get it?

But now I'm into the 3rd year of an accounting degree and I'm starting to realise it's not what I really want.

And the reason is that I didn't define that success on my own terms. I chose to do what others expected of me rather than finding out for myself what I really wanted.

And that's not the right way to do it.

"Approval from others doesn't guarantee success or happiness. It guarantees nothing. Sometimes it guarantees that you'll be miserable."

What does "success" mean to you? Don't know? Start finding out and get busy achieving it.

As Paulo Coelho has said in his book The Alchemist:

"When you want something, all the universe conspires in helping you to achieve it."

Don't waste that on achieving something you don't actually want.

Constantly Improve

Success is not about doing more, it's about being more.

You cannot expect to live the life you want to live by showing up today as the same you that you were yesterday.

Living the life, you want live means evolving every day into that person you want to become.

This is not for the weak minded. Evolving is hard.

You don't have to look into too many figures to find that out. Most people aren't reading books, working out, or even eating healthy.

And that's why most people will never be truly successful or live the life they want to live.

To get that you've got to constantly improve and watch as your mindset begins to expand, the world begins to bend to and you start to thrive.

All because you're making it happen for yourself.

As per William Faulkner,

"Always dream and shoot higher than you know you can do. Do not bother just to be better than your contemporaries or predecessors. Try to be better than yourself."

Act as if and Soon You Will Become

As per Jordan Belfort,

"Act as if! Act as if you're a wealthy man, rich already, and then you'll surely become rich. Act as if you have unmatched confidence and then people will surely have confidence in you. Act as if you have unmatched experience and then people will follow your advice. And act as if you are already a tremendous success, and as sure as I stand here today—you will become successful."

To live the life, you want to live you have to believe you're capable of living such a life.

That's the first step.

The second is constantly acting in a way that aligns with that belief. Doing so you'll soon see the exact results you want, become the person you want to be, and live the life you want to live.

I hope you'll do the same in your pursuit of achieving what you want to achieve.

"Progress is impossible without change, and those who cannot change their minds cannot change anything."

Most people won't ever live the life they want to live.

Their version of success isn't their own, and they'll likely never reach it.

They aren't evolving into a new version of themselves every day, and they're stuck with limited believes that will see them never act in a way that aligns with the person they want to become.

Don't be that person. Don't be content to stay where you are.

Define your own success, constantly improve, act as if you're living the life you want to live, and soon you'll be living just that.

As It Is and Let Go of What You Cannot Control

It's a given, we want to control the irrepressible parts of our life, believing we will attain happiness then.

I liken the thought to catching fireflies at night, certain you have caught them all. It is only later you realise there are more around and so you concede defeat.

I wish to emphasise one important key principle in this article. The rest is details:

Happiness = Accepting what is and letting go of what you cannot control.

It sounds simple right?

Then why aren't we happy?

Because what looks easy is often difficult to apply in real life. We want happiness to fill a void in our lives, but we don't want the struggle and difficulties that go with it.

Yet the pain and struggle serve as a reminder to stop influencing circumstances beyond our control.

I often remind others to stay in your lane. Meaning, you have no business poking around in matters outside your control because life is bigger than you and will impose itself upon you each time.

It has many millennia of experience and a toolbox of tricks, compared to your humble few decades of life.

"If you believe the outer circumstance is yoked inevitably to your story about it, then you will surely be at the mercy of whatever is going on in your life,"

I've researched countless books on happiness over the past decade, including attending seminars by respected psychologists and concede that happiness is much simpler than we think. Whilst I do not discount their tireless work and research, I am of the opinion happiness is accessible once our thoughts are in harmony.

It is our thinking that gets in the way of achieving happiness, not having a bank account full of money, fancy cars or luxury homes. Whilst these are good things to have, they wear off after a while and are meaningless if you cannot find peace and contentment within.

The Meaning You Give Your Experiences

Man is responsible for his problems because he creates them through his thoughts. Nothing outside you has meaning save for the meaning you give it. Your brain assigns meaning to life's events to make sense of what takes place.

"Meaning equals emotion and emotion equals life. The meaning you give your experiences will always change how you feel—and the emotion you feel always becomes the quality of your life."

Yet the meaning you give can be inaccurate if viewed through a distorted lens. For example, if you've been cheated on in a relationship, the meaning you ascribe to future relationships will be based on a lack of trust. This is neither right nor wrong, but one aspect of the picture.

Your happiness lies in reframing events to accept what is and let go of what you cannot control.

Referring to our earlier example where your trust was squandered through infidelity, the lesson gained is that you are likely to choose a trustworthy partner in your next relationship, given its relationship to your happiness. Contrast helps to shed light on what you value most and will be important to you.

To further emphasise the point, you accepted your previous partner's transgression, noting you may have played a role in co-creating an unbalanced union.

Note, I am not implying you consented to the unfaithfulness, however as a complying party you are still responsible for the events that took place.

Therefore, your lesson is to accept the dissolution of the relationship and release all judgement, anger and hate by healing and forgiving yourself and your former partner.

"Change the changeable, accept the unchangeable, and remove yourself from the unacceptable."

To continue harbouring anger and resentment ties you to the other person and does little to help you heal. In fact, you are likely to bring the toxic emotions into the next relationship, repeating the damage of the past and labelling future relationships as toxic.

"Reframing is the difference between being constantly disappointed and being consistently satisfied."

Amid the backdrop of acceptance is the invitation to let go of what you cannot control.

In this example, you cannot control other people's actions.

You cannot control whether they will return your love.

You cannot control if they will be faithful to you.

However, you can control your response to what happens.

You can control the meaning you give to the event.

You can control the lessons gained from the experience and carry them into the next relationship.

You can control whether you remain a victim or an ambassador for inner peace and harmony. These are powerful lessons, yet we ruminate on what went wrong in the past rather than how to carry the lessons forward.

"We are made wise not by the recollection of our past, but by the responsibility for our future."

I'm not saying it is easy and it may take years to achieve. It is a more worthwhile path than being a victim to your circumstances.

It is a given whilst we cannot control the circumstances of life, we can control how we respond to what happens to us.

This is a measure of our commitment to accept life as it is and let go of what we cannot control.

"So, in short as the title says – Be What You Are"

Acknowledgements

I would like to thank all the readers who are reading my books as they given me chance and motivation to write better.

Special thanks to my parents and my family for always being constant companion in supporting me in ups and downs.

Thanks to Microsoft Office 2010 as its really improved to find the spelling and grammatical mistakes easily.

Thanks to my Dell laptop for being running throughout my journey of writing this book.

And in the end thanks to the Almighty God for always there for showing me path.

Please read my book "Some Untold Chapters" which is real life inspired story of young boy Ravi and his story of belief and self motivation.

This was my first attempt as a motivational writer hope you like it, please provide your suggestions at –

abhinandan.asthana@gmail.com

<u>About the Author</u>

Abhinandan Asthana is an Engineer by profession and writer by passion. He has written three books till date on Technical Topics for Embedded Software Professionals.

Also he is author of famous fiction novel "Some Untold Chapters"

He belongs to the city of Temples and Ghats Varanasi.

His hobby was writing right from his college days and even he won title of "The Next Chekhov" in his college days while working he has started writing again in 2016, with technical books and this book is his first fiction novel.

Hope you all like it.

www.ingramcontent.com/pod-product-compliance
Lightning Source LLC
Chambersburg PA
CBHW050759240726
48654CB00008B/561